COLD SONGS

Dometa Brothers

Ice Cube Press, LLC
North Liberty, Iowa

Ice Cube Press, LLC (Est. 1993)
205 N. Front Street North Liberty, Iowa 52317
www.icecubepress.com steve@icecubepress.com
twitter: @icecubepress

The paper used in this publication meets the minimum requirements of
the American National Standard for Information Sciences—Permanence
of Paper for Printed Library Materials, ANSI Z39.48-1992.

Dedication

For my family who have loved me.

Also, for my teachers who heard the music in my
words and trained me to sing.

Contents

Bright Moon/Dark Water

Oracles of Winter

Tonight there is no moon—
only the empty vault of night.

The pale curve will not
entangle itself in the black, random—
but ordered—
silhouette of the trees.

The window frame will not show
the string of the moon meeting
the bow of your shoulder at the intersection
of inside and outside.

Only opaque night, black branches,
an empty Delphic darkness.

On the Banks of the Wolf River

I.
People pent in cities, or even medium size towns,
know nothing of darkness.
There, streetlights, headlights, the great nighttime
blaze of the car dealerships,
mute or even erase the flickering infinity
of the night sky.
They cannot see that stars are shifting silver wells and
occasionally rubious argent.
They have never lain on their backs by moving water
and seen the figures
wheel through the blackness—sky above moving
like water below.
They know stars do, move, of course, but they have to believe
a book or a teacher's word for it.

II.
On a heat thickened summer night when I was eight,
I rose when the house was sleeping
and followed the siren call of the frogs and crickets
to the banks of the river.
The horizon was bearing the weight of a low, heavy moon.
every star was more than doubled,
shimmering and bouncing off the eddying
water so that I barely
needed the light of a purloined flashlight.
I chose a circle of stamped-down grass where

whitetails had bed down before.
Muskrats, ungainly on land, slid sylph-like
into the water.

III.
The cliché is that rivers are like time. They aren't.
Rivers are about space, the obscure diffuse headwater
and the tail whipping its way into the ocean, the length,
the widening and narrowing breadth, the bright surface
and dark beneath, the inside and out, the bank and the water,
the trees and the reeds.

Rivers are not about your identity. They just aren't.
You cannot pin your own reflection on the surface.
If you are lucky, you can see some distance down
to fish, or weed, or rock. These creatures and things
are not about you.

IV.
Where the river turned past Strong's old place,
the ground became a flattened plain for more
than a mile—a broad swamp. The swamp
was for adventures. The collecting of tadpoles
was serious stuff. If you could bring them in
every stage, you were the science teacher's
Favorite.

The swamp is one of nature's fractals.
all points look remarkably similar. Each scraggly
cedar tree growing from raised moss covered clump

of barely holding on earth, each bed of cattails
swarming with small flies, each intermittent group
of delicate purple and gold irises, look exactly
like the repeated pattern.

My mother told me, "Don't only watch the ground
when you are walking. Check the sun." She packed
me lunches of sandwiches and equipped me with pails
and spades and mason jars with holes in the lids.
She told me, "If you think you are lost, especially
if it's getting dark, find the driest place handy and sit
down and wait." She showed me how to waterproof
my boots with mink oil. She told me, "If you get stuck
for more than a day, cattail roots are edible." She
never told me not to go. I don't think it
even crossed her mind.

V.
On crisp mornings the water leaves the river,
settles on surrounding soil, condenses in tiny
pools in the cleft uniting leaf to stem—forms
even on the living. Dew crusts dragonfly wings
like iridescent Austrian crystals; tops the tips
of muskrat hairs like scepters; makes a fine film
on my face.

The World Breathes Out

Outside, by the pond, now dark,
the linnets land causing the mild
water to move outward in tiny shock
waves. Each ripple meets others and their
combined forces pulse against the shore
causing the cattails to quiver like
a mouse's nose. Beneath,
the fish slip between roots beating
water, emptying their breath to mingled
movement.

Inside, I lie quietly, and try
to make my mind dormant
in a still, mute, shell. But the night
air carries a chorus of noise:
frogs, birds, crickets, toads, sing out
in euphonious cacophony. The air skims
my body raising tiny hairs, trembles
in my ear.

These metronomes of moments
mark movement.

The Seal

They've closed the bay.

There's a 45 mile wide sheet of ice clogging
the exit. Seven big freighters downbound
to mills in Gary, Chicago, and Detroit
are locked helpless—as frozen as human sound
on this desert.

The lead ship *Mackinac* had rammed forward
attempting to throw herself on nature's mercy,
meaning to crush that windrowe with the weight
of iron ore in her belly. She sits atop in humility—
a failure.

The six behind are duly chastened, two (whose
sailors breathe in sighs of relief) are still at dock.
There, night will be warm, with taverns and women
close to hand. But the great roar of the clock
of inward leaning ice

draws the other men from their beds to deck.
The ice blindly, apathetically, inexorably asserts
itself against the hulls. This thunder on earth
makes a measure of men and their tender hearts
that fear the worst.

The cutters will come when they can, but

it may be too late. The windrowes are high
with barricades of ice, strengthened by the air
and former snowfalls and melts: the refrozen, nigh
impossible to break.

By day six I see the helicopters suspending
their lines and baskets bringing food for
those men on the cutters who for seventeen
hours at a stretch canon water at the windrowes
to weaken them.

The noise inside the engine rooms booming,
mind maddening, repetitive, eruptions as
the cutters reverse battering ram style into the
thickened sheets of water, each great lurch the cause
of men knocked to their knees.

At night, after class, we gather on the bridge,
We wave at merchant marines and coastguard
men in their wool coats. By now they cheer
our arrival and red bandanas flutter rearward
in assurance.

Tonight the sky respects their efforts in
blazing show. The wavering curtains of green,
gold, and cerise, haunt the distant skyline of Duluth,
the city lights being no match for the scene—
the arctic apparitions overhead.

Here we are far from the traffic; we hear
nothing of vehicles. The magnetic display
haunts us in this present, no specter required.
Streamers of light arc wildly, violet at play
With puce sun particulates.

Suddenly, silence. We are not talking to each
other and waving to sailors. All turn to the sky
pageant, this passion play of ether. What absence.
The cutter has stopped its incessant cacophony
as men's eyes and hearts twist upwards.

The movements of God,
or sky, or world, take
all thought, seal all human sound,
as the light dances to silence.
It's April on the lake.

Wabi-Sabi

Surrounded by darkness
after the gluttonous bounty
of spring and early summer,
sheltered by the shadow of leaf,
steeped in darkness,
swaddled by the golden fruit
of its own body,
as the contents of self
reorganize—
establishing a new context:
this stomach shrinks here;
there, aptly named imaginal cells
bloom from near nothing to sensors
of air and movement; here,
they blossom to the flights of fancy.

Surrounded by darkness,
steeped in darkness,
inured to darkness,
Actia Luna emerges
to briefest beauty,
luminous in the dense night.

Over

I'm shaking, rattling, and rolling over
the Blatnik Bridge. Although it's three P.M.
the sky is densely dark and clouds roil,
so does the black water of Superior below.
I have to hurry before they shut her down.

There is a vertiginous quality here, suspended
between water and sky. The sheets of rain
further confuse the driving mind. I have to hurry
before they shut her down. The lightening burns

in sheets and those sheets burn with jagged
blasts as the rain tears open the sky. The dual waters
yearn desperately to be united. I, like Moses, have to
hurry before they shut her down.

Last year, last year, there was the car, the mind,
that lost its place in the liminal space of the bridge,
between the waters above and the waters below,
swept off the side like rain. I have to hurry.

White

The snow swirls down through moonlight, streetlight,
windowlight settling in opalescent folds between hills,

drifts up along the trees—rising,
climbing the darkened bark's crevices.

On this white world a stain is impossible.

Put down your papers. Leave your desk.
I'll gather your whiteness in my sun-dark arms as

the water-spun flowers of night fall, float, fly
animated—each a silvered slivered melting jewel.

Look here at the window above you:

The flowers recreate themselves on glass—
Transparency wedded to transparency—illumined in the firelight

of our room. I'll trace the seed of your soul
under the translucent skin of your collarbone.

Settle here in the sheet's white folds while

the wind builds
and the cloud-dark moon sets
more and more and yet more crystal
bud drops to fill the vale.
Undulating drifts
around an uncertain center
swell and slope paper white against storm
darkened earth.

There

—arrange the blanket—

sink against the crook of my arm.
Outside the storm subsides.

The wind eddies; the first light shines
through annealed bride-blossomed-windows.

Pothos

To hell with serenity,
I want joy.
And so, as morning comes
with a languid orange light—I
prepare my feet with boots and hands with gloves.
I drink my tea scalding to carry
some warmth with me in my belly

and I walk out into the January
world. The air crystalizes in my throat
and barely reaches my lungs in solid form.
But, the cold is a brilliant conductor
and I hear the singing
souls of sleeping animals.
Beside the river, I
can hear the song of the water
rushing below the ice.
Like me; locked in matter.

I sink into the drift of the bank
because nothing burns like snow.
I sing the song of cold.
The fire of cold will reveal
that this drift is desire,
Here, nascent truths coalesce
into my second, white, shadow.

Diane and Mnemosyne

Reared in the country, far from the comforting pools
of light cast by the city street lamps, one learns
to love the dark. I walk out into darkness
unafraid.

I wash myself in the liquid black of night
and sew it up inside my body's pockets
to dampen my heart with later.

Tonight, the moon, low and heavy
like a pregnant belly, is trapped in the black
branches of trees, but also,
the black river of night. It has been so
on many wanderings out and back. I
have told the doctors so.

Yes, the moon/dark river is a metaphor
(meta: above or over, pherein: to bear across).
I am not the moon. I am not the darkness.

The richness of a dark night: the mist of moonlight
coating the dense air like the pale bloom on a dark
sweet plum, reveals a tiny, wee, toad on the path—
no bigger than my pinky nail. The beating
of wings, like whispers, are portents of the outcome.

The moon has pressed 'round me, followed me
into my room and back out again, settled in
the creases of my neck, made silver pools in my
navel, and dust flecked the irises of my eyes.

That moon, (or maybe another), leans heavily
against the sturdy branches of oaks. It has
bounced there off the points of the pines.
Oak trees, like small children with balloons,
know the importance of not letting go.

It is not ascending, not tonight anyway. But,
how I have wished to not be a favorite of the moon.
I would have changed magic for reason; I would
have carved her into such small, manageable, bites.

Only the inhuman love of the trees holds her.

Winter People

People

live in
the great spaces
between
each other
and
they
die there, too.

Cabin Fever

There was a girl whose body became
a piece of flesh strange to her, behind whose eyes
lay snow fields. She lost all surprise
and delight at thresholds.

All things became weird (in the old sense).
The sofa fabric's grey nubby slubs,
startled and repelled her. The empty washtubs
in the laundry room, a horrible abyss.

She lost herself in the clean hallways
of home, the dust motes' silent dance
a memory of crystals settling a scant
distance to smooth stone.

It was not the need to get out. Indeed,
it was the not getting out, out—the reality
too close—the strange interior melody
of snow and cold.

The Edges

We played by the pond—scrupulous
to stay on the side away from the beaver
family, all happily paddling, diving, returning
to the woods' edge. Meanwhile, within sight
of us and the house, you
worked steadily, slowly pushing
the heavy logs through the splitter,
piles of fluffy sawdust
and a neat stack of cordwood rising.

A wave of your hand would send
us to the garage to divest ourselves
of muck covered swimsuits, ready ourselves,
for shredded pork sandwiches and creamy
pea salad. You and the Mrs. and your three and
me. And me, I waited for the prayers to
end. The quiet purpose of the words
thrilled and scared me like your
voice rising softly as pipe smoke from
the red leather chair after supper.

One afternoon, while you wheeled
barrows of dirt and moved timbers
to where nasturtium and lilies would
later delight, you retrieved your camera
and lined us girls like a foreshadowing
of hollyhocks.

Through the years, I've come to know
that you were the fuel
that warmed that house,
the soil that made the flowers bloom.

The first good man I ever knew.

Like Mars

North Dakota is a different kind of cold,
a treeless cold. No pine trees to buffer
the howl, no undergrowth to absorb the bitterness.
Even "winter wheat" must be planted with the cover
of stubble from a previous crop. The standing dead
remainders help collect snow. A million seeds
per acre planted in September, with just the right
amount of rain, a propitious blanket of snow
on the stubble guarding potential life,
may allow some to resurrect in Spring.

A friend from North Dakota said,
"It's a good place to be *from*." He smiled
and took a long drag off his cigarette,
"It gets colder there than some places
on MARS. I started smoking to feel
some warm air in my lungs." He hesitated,
and added, "If Jesus were born
in North Dakota, our vision of hell
would be empty cold."

Keeping Time

Your little hands
dishevel birch saplings, first
bending them to the ground,
and then,
whip-snap letting them go. Only
your laughter flies faster
than the whippet of branches
cutting air slicing
my heart, as
my tiny moon travels
so far from my body.

Cutting Brush

Early morning and early evening were
the times for her attack. The heat was
subdued, but the insects were not.
She started in early spring;
she raged until late fall.

Out came the loppers, weed whacker,
hacksaw, and occasionally, a small,
plug-in chainsaw. With netting over
her head, goggles over eyes, pants
tucked into boots, and long leather gloves,
she went to battle. She was Metis varying her
defense and form. She cursed
the hazel brush encroaching on the west
side flower beds. She was tormented by
the spring poplars that seemed, like Athena,
to suddenly emerge fully grown—desperate
for war.

Long before she knew what lurked,
she lunged and parried. Hours, days,
years, were devoted to the advance. Then
out would come herbicides, landscaping
fabric, and trowels for a change of engagement.

Unbeknownst to her, a small dark spot
went undetected, it too sent threads in

compound attacks on all fronts.
She plucked and pulled and chopped, making
sunshine for the flowers, lilies and lupines, and
topsoil for the potatoes and corn. But the deep world
of the forest would advance. It sent its dark shoots
snaring her, it moved through her blood,
in an enveloping corps-a-corps.

Then one fall morning, harvesting corn, she
fell to the ground with the worst headache
of her life. There would be no reprise.

Years later, the house is long gone;
there where it was, and beyond
into the garden space, and yet beyond,
are an open field of royal colored lupine
and coral daylilies. They have naturalized—
taken over the yard, the crumbling foundation,
obscured the driveway. They extend past
the edge of the tree line, pushing into the undergrowth.

Transplant

He can't see the words before him,
"You're in my light," he says glancing up.
She talks slowly now, like she moves,
"I need...some help outside."
He scowls, but it is play, as he
looks over his glasses,
"I thought we agreed that this
gardening was your hobby."
"But...there's...a root, a big root."

He pushes away the crossword puzzle and
slowly lifts his height to tower over her.
He places one hand on her back guiding her
toward the door. As they step out
onto the porch, the hand steadies her in the bright
white glare. She leads him to under the tree
by the low stone wall.

There before him is the site: the sod
peeled back, the exposed root
with the evidence of her assault marring
nothing but the topmost layer
of its thinnest portion. Waiting near
are the smaller, drooping, plants—
pale green streaking the darker spears.

The root is twisted; and at its thickest, it crosses

back onto itself.   Her small trowel is wholly
inadequate to the task. He toys with the disturbed moss
and asks, "Why do they have to go here? Two feet
over—no problem." She settles herself on the low wall,
"They've grown too thick…by the house…
they must be moved…they'll starve themselves…
And die there by the wall."
"Okay, but why not there, or there, or anywhere
but directly over this damned root system."
"They need shade…to protect them
from the sun. They'll burn in the sun; some
things need shade."

With the finality of her words, he rises
to his height and descends the path leading
into the garden shed, disappearing into its black
center. In a few long moments he is back—
carrying a larger spade whose edge gleams in bright stark
contrast to the darker, duller, bowl.
His full weight leans onto the top edge
of the shovel, again, again, again, until
the root looks like a mighty rope frayed
in the center.

He wipes the sweat out of his eyes, growls
low swear words, and glances at her implacable face.
He knows he must finish this task. He feels
her urgency for the small plants that wait, thirsty
for water, and shade, and space.
In desperation, he stoops low, grabs the spade

with both hands and with the full force of his arms,
back, and chest, strikes the root at it's now weakened center.
It snaps. She smiles. He swears as the sting
of his sweat and blood drip onto the cool
damp earth.
She says nothing, but places the new plants
tenderly, carefully, in their prepared place.
He has moved back to the house and the silhouette
of his frame swells the doorway. He knows
when her charges are safely restored that
she will come to him, rinse cool water
over the wound, uncurl his palm, and in the shadow
cast by her face and hair, will breathe a kiss onto the sacrifice.

Winter People

On the street in town, are all the winter people.
The girls vanish to nothing under scarves, caps, coats,
until they seem no more than pale mouths
and eyes.
From every direction they float along the black
ice of the pavement. They struggle against the
blank air,
their garments all varieties
of brown and grey and black—dark
winter flowers.
The men are all made of frigid, solid air,
skating across this treeless landscape,
hats hovering above collars,
empty gloves clutching their suits about them—
graves walking.

Duluth's Persephone

It was the kind of hopeless cold
that makes buildings seem
miles away.

The iron grey sky,
ruthlessly pulled tears
from the edges of his eyes.
Cold pressed him
deeper into the depths
of dark coat, scarf, and thoughts.

Crossing the expanse
between buildings –
under a white distant, sun—
then, a miracle.

There she was

at the top of the steps leading to the library,
pomegranate red jacket open,
long, warm, yellow hair escaping cap, and cloak, and scarf,
head thrown back,
laughing at January.
The solid dome of frigid sky splintered.

Linger: Proprioceptive Halo

Today is a day to linger
over tea, while the sun burns off the breakfast fog;
here at this kitchen table I touch the cold morning glass
of the window overlooking the back yard, blending
almost imperceptibly with the field, fading to wood.
There is something, a lump, lodged in my throat.

The majestic cardinal preens
his scarlet feathers. The rabbit's
grazing is punctuated by the intermittent thrusting of his head—
the hypervigilance he carries in the pit of his stomach.
October sun warms the last aerial feats
of the butterfly.

To linger
I watch the steam from my refreshed cup
rise sinuously, twining with the "babies"
of the spider plant. The leaves will settle
it like interior dew, drawn in and up.
You are not home. You are somewhere, in the back of my
mind.
We can't be everywhere. That's why there is space.

Before us, or this kitchen though,
there have been many October mornings,
alike and different, with patches of scarlet
and fur and air moving over everything.

Once, somewhere, I am ten, waiting
(was waiting) for the bus. This morning
I waited in the magic of hoarfrost
formed straight from ephemeral sky to solid crystal.
Air moved over my face and tried to draw crystals
from my eyes and lips and breath as well.

The sky burst with the wave of crashing
noise--the metal I heard twisting, but,
did not see. The vital heat of blood rose in me
As I ran down the road, around the corner where
trees gave way to corn fields. One straggling
tree had absorbed the body of a car.

The body of the car had absorbed the body of a man.

I bent over the other body, a yearling doe,
under whose head bloomed molten roses.
A twitch across her face I thought I felt,
her breath pushing into my hand, and I knew:
you are your barriers, skin outlining patch of earth.

Now here at this table waiting,
the sun warms the October world beyond the window, limbering
the beat of a butterfly's wings like the breath of time.
I rise, the carrion inside of me.

Baking Bread

The young wife rises with the dawn of mid-September
while her husband's form lingers in the liminal space of dreams;
she patters to the kitchen and retrieves the recently acquired
cookbook. Her finger slides along the index. She remembers

his exclamatory nostalgia of a soft-pillowed morning
and the rousing, wavering, aroma of bread that nudged
him down boyhood stairs toward the practical embrace
of a farmhouse woman. The encomiums to melting

butter. Her assemblage of ingredients is hap-hazard
and betrays her awkward entrance to the novitiate.
She worries overmuch about the word "tepid"
in the recipe as she tips a spoonful of living yeast toward

the cup of water and sends up a prayer that she's right.
She ignores the curious word "sift" and transfers flour
from can to counter. A well is formed in the midst of the
wheat and three well-beaten eggs form a pretty yellow sight

in the circle of flour. The yeast is added to this slowly.
She uses her hands to combine the life of last year's
harvest, the living yeast, and the would have been living
eggs as they morph into something new. The dough, sticky

is kneaded to a dusty ball. Her now stained book intones
"remove dough to greased bowl and cover with clean towel."

This forgotten preparation is hurried through. The book
commands the lump be sheltered in warmth until grown

to twice its size. She waits in solemn silence in the still
dark kitchen, peaking under the towel after two slow hours
pass. The bubbling, living batter makes her wonder in deep
muteness. She cuts the dough in half and presses each until

they take the form of the waiting pans. The next part of an hour
is spent in the divided silence of the kitchen entranced as the loaves
rise again. Next she presides before the oven doors as the simple
lumps transform into the stuff of life under her small power.

He enters in time to see her graceful body sing
the song of offering and emerge with sun-colored,
lop-sided loaves. He asks "And what did I do to deserve
this great gift?" She answered, "Not a thing."

Between the Season

Spring Thoughts

These thoughts for worn out spring:

The muddy tracks, the branches spent in bloom, the stretching
of days
to the breaking point—

the sun, that old coin,
melts down to flood this terrestrial ball, and to dry, and to
scorch, and to blaze.

Trillium Grandiflorum

Once,
in late May,
in the Yosemite Valley,
in the Mariposa Sequoia Grove,
among great, grey, granite boulders,
I cowered,
surrounded
by the
spires
of a
natural
cathedral.

But, I found nowhere to fix my eyes, no center or locus of
meditation, only the majestic vertiginous. So unlike the woods
of my past selves, without the comfort of the holy homely—no
cover of overarching maple, no grotto of underbrush where
hazelnuts drop abundant gifts. No stream or spring bubbled in
that arid place to relieve a human thirst.

My heart and hands drift to the forest floor of memory,
where a carpet of white, and green, and gold, draws
my eyes down and inward. From the soft suede petals, three

white points toward a golden center where nectar draws
the tiny ants that will carry out acts of service to seed
yet more. Deeper, deeper, the single center but hints at laws

of multiplicity. The green extends beyond the earth to what lies beneath, to rhizomes connecting each to each, to earth and sky, and my breath escapes my body tumbling out like a cloud of butterflies.

Divine Mathematics:
Passion of the Pattern

Today, I am a necromancer of peonies.
They have died back, shriveling
from sky to loam.
Only the sere stubs and leaves withered in on themselves
remember
their recent sumptuous past.

A dream of the chaos of high summer,
their full blown symmetry and complex allure
of bloom and green belied
hidden order.

Then, the plants rose from the black earth
aspiring to sunshine—
each separate stalk, a radial axis upon which the leaves
form an efficient stage
for the play of sun and earth—
each single branch spiraling left or right,
according to the handedness of nature's daemon.

The globular blossom, *kephale* and *kardia*, drooped
with the weight of harmony.
Purfled petals soft as velvet feathers arranged themselves
whorls within whorls.

Now, all that symphony is quiet.

After shovel reveals the fleshy tubers,
I kneel, and extending both hands shake
the roots free of time.

I bring the rhizome to my sightline
looking eagerly for the "eyes" and
quickly sever
each from other.

Next, they will be re-interred across the yard
by the irises that my mother gave me,
as single type calling forth the manifold,
and as delicate pink counterpoint to the purple.

There, reborn, they may mark a century
of ever unfolding glory, a memory of the future.

The Abeyance

Summer is the season of clarity, where single leaves
seem stamped, no, lasered from the stuff of living.
There is no blurring, no obfuscation of the raw.
Where even the flower petal's ruffled edge
is clean, keen. Thousands of evergreen limbs
covered in thousands of tiny spears.
Grass is blades.

After a morning rain, the cleanness of the green
seems almost to slice the eye and heart that
beholds. Even the pond mirrors glass, as though
the bluntness of gazing could force a web
of cracks across the smooth surface, converting
fluidity to jagged edge—something to hold
in the hand gingerly, fiercely.

Integrity

It is not fear, exactly. Or, it is not only fear.
On a languid July day—all green and blue—
I flush with the heat of the sun, and, sitting here,
the lake should beckon with the promise of cool.

It is not only fear, but uneasiness. The lake
laps at the shore and swallows stray limbs
that fall and sink below surface. Watch it take
the water that small creek weeps into it.

Not only fear. It is a sort of silent distress
at the entering in. Even in winter, when
I walk across the lake's back, there is the stress
of breaking the integrity of the hard skin

of water and plunging through that boundary.
To jump from the rocks and jack knife into water
and pulsating weeds is disconcerting. Bloodthirsty,
to sink into the spongy bottom; a slaughter

to step, accidentally, on the crab excreting bone.
The water weeds have small defense, a transient melody
of touch and counter touch, a waving tactile moan.
The silver grey bullet fish brush by ineffectually.

Still, I am afraid. Terrified.

Great Lakes Fulgurite

My heart leaps out like wind,
caressing the stones, ascending I
sharpen myself on trees whittling
them to razor points until
the spark of my exertions ignite
the heavens—the dark dazzles.

I descend, absorbed back into earth
filling the spaces between sand,
whipping myself liquid and then
cooling solid to branches,
outside stony, inside,
clear as water—
like the wind.

Energy from the heavens
to hold in your hand,
embodied again in this earth.

Archimedes in Superior, Wisconsin

Mists lie on the fields like white
curls of cigarette smoke, as
yesterday dies with the gold
morning light.

The feel of the trace of breath
against a neck, like
palimpsest text spiraling lines
shadow depth.

And some roads go on and some roads turn back.

Roots snake between brick, fair
passage paused, since
rhizomat grass recovers
puzzle squares.

Bees pause before orange blossoms—
petals beckon, the
dynamic stall of floating
bodies' sum.

And some roads go on and some roads turn back,
and some lives go on without any tracks.

Autumn Songs

I. Bee Song: Outside Itself

Bees fly between raindrops
circumnavigating liquid globes,
each a deluge for the plump body, the legs no
thicker than a filament of hair.

The wing vibrates smoothly and rapidly,
delicate seeming veins and membranes,
a transparent tissue. No. The wings grow
from the materials of the exoskeleton.

Bee bone, carried outside itself, strong.

Each worker seeks a flower. One flower
succeeds another, again, again. Each offers slightly
altered nourishment. Each remarkably similar;
each wildly different.

 II. Orchard Song: Windfall

Apple trees in the orchard
are remarkably small. Grafted, manipulated,
stunted, but fecund.

On a bell shaped, blue sky day, we
slowly ascend the hill. I carry bags
to swell with fruit. You carry the baby.

Like some biblical giant
you can stretch your height to the top of every tree.
Your broad hand closes 'round white firm flesh—

the integrity assured by the
red and yellow striped skin. Each is inspected
for the desecration of insects.

One arm cradles the plump baby
while the other stretches out to me
a sphere, a globe—holding the promise

of next year's intended fruit
safely—yet now unfulfilled. I
place it into the bag's emptiness.
I carry a separate bag, stooping low, looking for windfall.
Some apples, still apparently perfect, lie
soft in the grass. Orchard staff
charge $1.99 a pound for apples plucked
from the trees' bodies and fifty cents for
nature's discard.

They know that the bruises will rise to the surface
—eventually—
they trust you to tell the truth at the scales.

The bags about to burst,
you hand me the baby,
And heft the now heavier bags for the slow descent.

A Symphony of Snow

There's a certain smell of autumn—
of rich, cold, and mouldering leaves.

But, not only that.
It is also the scent of hardy mums
eating oblique rays of sunshine.
Chrysos. The storing of the golden.
Not sweet, but herbaceous and peppery.

It is also, but not only, the perfume of
that sun soaked loam freezing at night
—by day—
releasing the imprisoned
back into the air: the incense of light.

There is a certain smell of autumn—
of expectation—
the scent of
crickets, tiny night birds,
slowing their song,
as the sky tunes.

The Gloaming

We are made to forget.
We are made for the slow dissipation of mists
and obfuscation.

Some sharp tree lines defy the glare of sun,
or, gloam-tinted branches break up the sky.

We, the hollowed out logs,
We, inside worn out unknowingly,
and filled with tomorrow's rain.

Heart Cycles

Love on the Plains

Outside the darkened Iowa sky is thick with rain.
Violet, violent heat traces sheets of energy from darkened sky
to darkened earth.

Somewhere beneath is the vague frightening blackness
of the river, shrunken back
from its banks—brief illuminations of fireflies.
Switchgrass, bluestem, and the honey locust quiver
under the weight of sky.

Inside we are carved earth and the breath of life.
Your mouth tastes like mine, and the shadow of light
hints at the trace of long form.

Beyond the strange doubleness of limbs
the air folds across our forms
—a complete space. There is living in the earth,
in the air. We are potential and kinetic energy.

In heavy doubled darkness,
bearing the weight of the horizontal sky,
swallowing traces of light,
the blossoms descend from the honey locust tree.

The Time It Takes Falling Bodies to Light

You lie in the grass with
beckoning, outstretched arms, palms up.
Dusk plays at shadow games tinging
the gold and green of grass with grey and purple.
The grey-green purple-gold grass mingles
with the shadowy copper of your hair.
Twin winged dragonflies shimmering emerald,
overcast in blue in this twilight haze float,
a troupe of marionettes, on clear,
violet dusk threads.

The gloaming blurs the edges of air,
of grass and hair,
of fingertips' rosy crests
emerging from the earth. At first a light play,
the red on red reveals itself a ladybeetle threading
its way from the blade's edge to the golden thread's way
toward your face.

I look down at the hovering wing's edge, the fluttering
shell or hair, the last lateral light of day playing
off your fingertips blooming in the grass.

I sink.

Heart Cycle

I. Landscape Epithalamion

Hearts and fingers around each other twirled
shuttling steadfast ties yet not encapsulating.
Dew dance leaving the flower heavy hung, empearled;
shades and types of glory—one and adumbrating.
Love's threading tendrils swirled
reaching in, singing, webbing through
the strands of our selves sympathetically vibrating
steeply inclining to a thing wholly new.

A grove of English elms' deep correspondence,
striking in recursive multiplicity
—happy in the fact of rooted singularity—
binary stars reaching out across the distance
each circling through our respective sky
and weaving a new heaven between us.

II. Forever Fleeing, Falling Back

Midnight's self holds the tightly furled
bloom of tomorrow in close, jet, hands
secreted like treasure between the eve and
morn. Dreams tease your eyes; your hands uncurl
and return. Your breath is but a shadow
of your spirit held fast over the abyss.
Forever fleeing, falling back with a low
promise of return—each a kept kiss.

And yet—treasures stored are treasures yet.
Morning's midnight's loss, and, dreams' mists
are nothing in the open hand. A part
of dreams prisoned over the precipice
lives. Pardon not the unpardonable—past selves
hover in the endless moment of the heart.

III. Of Good and Evil

Night held us both softly, warmly, safely,
before I taught you all about love lost—
your body, a strange small double, only
softer against my bent knees and shoulders—lost
in the endless return of past states, old minds,
former bodies' burning metamorphosis. Before I knew
that goodness lay in you like a pearl, to find
beneath your pale skin, a seeming shell of blue
veins, fragile web protecting, blanketing all life,
holding warmth closely, safely. So near to you.
But know, all distance is immeasurable. Now rife
with the knowledge that I can knead a pearl to
dust, your white beauty seems more fragile. I
return to feel your naked heart's ash drift by.

IV. Fragile Negotiation

These kitchen walls are yellow, but they
are creamy, buttery, not lemon. Bright
sun plays in patterns cast by the upright
ladder chairs. It is charming, but some say

small, cramped. But interior spaces can play
tricks on eyes, on minds, on hearts, until light
asserts its delicate virtue. The blight
of "cheap and cheerful" spreads decay

across kitchens, faces, cultures, and souls.
Yet, it has undeniable power to erase
the patina of worth across the whole
of two lives. Or more. You move to replace
the poppy covered mug with cream and rose
china, bringing me tea—improbable moment of grace.

V. Forgiveness

Unspoiled desire, a winter's tale of grandeur:
I, deciduous forest, holding a net of growing
against the sky. Great mountains rise rending
the green skin of earth, the jagged stones stir.
Each river stone is smoothed into a single, pure,
descended moon. You, water, fine mist rolling
against mountains, like tender rain showers, sing
the sharp cedar incense of woodsy air.

Breath of world in a first and only summer, kissed,
a space between. Then, such pain. Such pain
is a promise of love. And now, I, the mist
of steam weighting the seams of shirt as keen
as a knife's edge. You, the solid bricks,
up-built, surrounding our garden.
The truth is plain that now we know,

that love is desire's compassionate repose.

VI. The Last Love Song

Then, your eyes' twinned in mine, and mine in yours,
infinite regress on double pillowed mornings—
led me to believe that rooms daily course
with answering voices. The smile reflecting
in the mirror above the dresser adumbrates
Pythagoras' ethics of symmetries.
Your living force so permeates
these hollow chambers. The song decrees
I am the strange attractor whose face
calls forth specters in now empty bedrooms.
I'm left nosing darkest corners of the place,
seeking your voice in these now vacant rooms.

Surely your heart chambers' so sweet last sigh
must remain. Some echo. Some haunt. Some cry.

VII. Just Another Love Story

Mid-November's iron grey sky clamps poplars
and brown grassy fields tight with a binding
frost. In this trap, is the memory of spring's
eyes: stars behind still black rivers.
The winter fields devise decay. The soft
drift of snow muffles chaos. Here the crisp
autumn seed rests in soil and in grey-kissed
dreams, awaiting the sun-sweet defrost.

Winter, the time to burn the quick—when shadows
call back. But, how can I bear the memories
of past sweetness, here, in my bone-bound soul?
The polished skeletal wisdom of the body
whispers truth freshest summer does not know:
All love stories end the same; someone is alone.

In the Last Light of August

You came to me in the season of the purple flowers:
August, the summer's end, the beginning of autumn,
the close of season's day before the fractured light of dawn
in the perpetual mourning of winter.

We spread like the wildflowers along the roadsides
and meadows. The rosy purple clover carpeted the ground
with petals sweet as marrow and the chaos of wild
phlox waved to us from the wood's edge. We waved back
to ourselves, to the other.

Your pink, tiny, foot wandered to my thigh, cool
like the violet fairy slippers, woodland orchids.
The grand asters ascended heavenward against the weight
of dozens of royal-hued blooms, golden light
winking through them.

The hazy periwinkle sky above them and us was filled
with domes of nimbus, dusky ivory-grey before and
backlit with an amber aureole. There, we blossomed,
accompanied by the burgundy foliage
of the sedum singing—each of ourselves,
each for the other.

Love on the Lake (Apostle Islands)

We are recently returned from Mackinac Island where
the June air, though chilled, is oppressed by the heavy
perfume of lilacs—here, the more delicate scent a stair
of lupine, bloodroot, and tangles of wild, single, white roses.

The boat glides off the launch point at Raspberry Bay
into the dark, clear, water of the Big Lake. Morning light tricks
fold off waves making tiny rainbows as the last of grey
night evaporates. Soon the metamorphosis

from lake to sky will complete itself. In the boat
you shift side to side, the newest lateral rays of sun
forming a halo of light against your solid figure, the rote
movements, a memory of strong arms. Most

of my sightline is swollen with you and your memories
until we round the tip of Devil's island. Here the sandstone
cliffs are layers of copper and bronze. Light bends and ellipses
around wave carved reentrants—sun tinted pillars, burning
souls

before heaven. You slide the boat cleverly before the west
wall reentrant, so narrow we are forced to grasp
the sides of the sandstone cave with both arms. Without rest
we ease and angle the boat some minutes. Close

to exhaustion in the dark, close, cave I move with you

but without seeing you, trusting your movements as my own.
The boat rocks against walls until we emerge into
a flood of light. The cool waters blaze aureous

as I see the sanctuary,
a nave gifted by lake
and land and sky—
and my heart folds into a rose.

What Angels Know

Cold Implements

Winter wind is
thick like air impasto.
It lays on the surfaces
of trees and buildings until
the sky boldly moves
the solid sculpture in furrows
of grey, with reflections
of dove and cream.

Winter wind carves out
the landscape, the rent wing feathers
of small snow birds, the lines across
cheeks and at the corners of eyes, the cracks
incised in winter-sky colored barn wood—
Intaglio, where the cold can drop
and settle and can
never be completely
wiped away.

The Goodness of the End of Things: Thoughts from Hawai`i

The earth, eroded volcano,
mounds invitingly over feet, soft and fine like caster sugar,
warm with the memory of the center of the earth—
warm, warm, warm—sometimes
inhospitably hot.

It is not like the cool black earth
of windswept Iowa, prairie grass claiming
its own—the roots holding on
to the dessicated remains of
seasons past.

It is not like the cold blasted sand and clay
of Wisconsin earth. Scraped out by glacier,
hardened and unyielding
to the efforts of the machinery—resistant to welcoming
my grandmother's body
back home.

The earth here is beautiful.
churned from the core, rising up
from the blue-green depths,
annealed by fire,
polished by sea,
resplendent with verdure and color...

…always warm.

Tomorrow, I will leave this place.
The stephanotis vines, their blooms flowering
spectacularly near the surface
of this volcanic earth, will close at night—
without me to mark the moment of the loss of their perfume.
There is a goodness to grief, to the end of things.
Surely God has touched this earth, lit it ablaze with beauty;
touched it, but, He has not tempered it.

Fascination with Infinity

There aren't proper words for cold.
Stingy words. Barren words.

Even if there were,
we're not allowed to have them.
The words and the cold.

We are all fighting the cold.

Once, I saw a girl whose eyes
were like a green spring leaf
under the frozen layer of a bird bath.

Theirs was a kind of creeping cold.
We're all fighting the cold.

Our eyes seek and search other eyes.
Our eyes sound out the stars
across all that blue cold.

Cold is a filling, satisfying, thing.
Words are tiny, quiet, and quite retold.

Think of the terribleness of the absence of cold.
How a splendid vermillion sun
begins to waver and shimmer and become untold,

evaporating text in the absence of cold.

Meanwhile

Those stars (tiny things to cold) not speaking to us
(perhaps long dead) –as time folds—
seem to endlessly dip and ellipse
strategically, silently, endlessly rolled
across that vaster real manifold—
expanding red-shifting humanity eclipsing bold
realm of star-making word-breaking all-enfolding vellum
stretch of cold.

In your immense black pupils
the interstellar blast.
The deep darkness of God.
The reality of cold.

Come Close, I'll Whisper a Secret

Hell is for people who refuse to see beauty, who
with eyes clenched tight (and fists too)
deny its existence. People who see wombs
full of worms and their slickened trails.

People who refuse to honor *gravitas,*
the descent into things—they see only
velvet petals. But even the hothouse rose
cradles a memory of wildness. It knows

the trail of worms and the marks of weather
create it anew—it yearns to be beaten by rain
and made sere by snow and withered back to
the tears inside, to shrink under the blue

sky. Such movement provokes denial though.
To see inside past all—to the secret silence—is to go
past the velvet, the world, the rain,
the dessication, and the pain.
It is to know; it is to know,
the secret of beauty:
The sacredness of tears in things,
the magic empty spaces.

More

I am half sick of brown bird beauty
and all that is austere.
I want, I want to fall
more. Just more
of everything. But most of all
to see hear taste touch move more.

I am dying for a cosmogony of senses
—some articulated accent of red tulip,
caterpillar hair soft folds barely concealing
some guiled sweet gatherer's sip.

No more bare beauty. I want none of it.
Which is just what there is
to have

to have some unashamed
mystic divine something
something grand beyond grand
and
some stars—some unnamed constellations scattered—a dew
from heaven's dark firmament—competing.

Competing. Yes! Competing pageantry.

I want a riot.

Cascades of everything! Let there be
bowers burdened with burgundy roses
falling
to soaked earth heavy with the smells
of rain, roses, smoldering skies
like
the filaments of green blue gold
spun from the aureole,
reflected in your sea glass colored eyes.

A mind maddening reflection,
an infinite regress
multiple, mobiacal, madness

I want

To mark the movement, all
movement, from the hush of your
eyelashes breathing life
into the mound of my cheek, falls
To
the thrumming, pulsing movement
of my heart, your blood,
our undiluted souls incandescent—
in the bump a bump pulse of a wrist
more cataracts without, within

I want to fall
—find reason—
to reach and rend

something remarkable—

Remarkable. Something, some muse
I want
to open—to unfold—
a thousand satin ribbons
like
the tight lilac fuse
bursting.

Inside Outside

The drift is white; but it is not white.
Solid; but mostly space. To scoop
a handful up is to handle infinity. Once
upon a black cloth or clear glass slide is
how the fantastical narrative unwinds.

The hand can contain a million miniature
sculptures clear as glass, as water, as air
in the diffusion of light. The intricacies
of delicate worlds so easily invisible—
the light they reject.

Their clarity is a wonder. Things to see
and things to see through. To discover
each is also a way of seeing out and in
simultaneously. Tiny descended star within

infinity. Hexagonal water flowers, each
growing across worlds. Impossible
works of art, wrought for whom? The thoughts
are as dizzy as the actions of this super cooled
earth-cloud. Each existing, vast spaces within them.

What Consumes Man

I.
Deep in the interior of this beaux arts temple
rising from the prairie, in a labyrinth of galleries,
past the interior courtyard, beyond the baroque paintings
(appropriately displayed on deep red walls), is a miracle.

Wrought by an 18th century Italian artist forgotten
by history, or never known, is "The Fall of the Rebel Angels."
The entire sculpture is 10 inches by six. A knot,
a mass, of tiny figures carved from ivory
(hundreds maybe, too confusing to count), in combat

for heaven. At the apex the Trinity, seated, calm
expressions meticulously carved on faces a few
millimeters wide; not far below, off center, is Michael
the archangel, sword aloft in the charge against myriad demons.

The demons are largely naked: their protruding sternum
matched with knobby horns, stunted wings, and stringy arms.
Each twists wildly, simultaneously engaged in battling and
plummeting.
The angels are smooth-skinned, clothed in impossibly fluid,
ivory,
garments. Their arms (and where exposed in battle) legs, slen-
der yet brawny, tiny
articulated muscles surging in the fight. Destruction wrought
with tridents, subdued by staffs.

The fight intensifies traveling downwards. Toward the middle
the minute facial expressions of the angels are grimaces of
effort, making it difficult to tell fallen
from victors. But, toward the horrors of the bottom, terror
again differentiates
the visages. The rebels tumble, some headlong with mouths
gaping grotesquely. Others fall, clutching and clawing upward,
into the mouth of the waiting serpent. As in Dante's *Inferno*,
Satan endlessly devours those who served him—each a
delicacy of pride.
The infinitely complex figures and details draw the viewer, like
the rebels, inconsolably into the grisly scene of the universe in
the bell jar.

II.
Stepping out into the sunlight onto the large court
just beyond the museum doors, viewers are confronted
with Rodin's "Thinker." The seated bronze raised
on stone plinth, beyond life-size, demands rapport.

The rugged beauty, again, of thighs, calves, broad back,
but in repose. The study for a piece never finished:
"The Gates of Hell." Rodin died, frozen in unheated
quarters during the war. The works, safe from attack,

recently gifted to the embattled state, snug, in the warm fold
of the Museum. Thought of the doorway surround with a tiny
"Thinker" at its crest contemplating the fates of the souls
of men, is occluded by the sight of this monolithic entity.

We are frozen—absorbed, drawn down,
into the solid bronze heart of man.

III.
Shuttlecocks, levity included,

scatter wildly   no,   langorously
across the garden grounds

                                        leading to

The City

                          comfy classy (but no! never elitist!)
Claus/Coosje

Oddly,   archaic sport, so delicate it was played   indoors
(?).

20 foot toys

dropped
                                        hurriedly

by giants

as

interest

wanes.

Oddly

Doors fascinate. And not just beautiful ones,
covered in delicate carvings, or magnificent
ones like the museum doors with bronze
surrounds, each an exquisite molded narrative.
But all true solid doors, especially odd
doors. Doors of strange sizes
leading to strange places, spaces.
Old, black, cast iron coal doors
in the Victorian masonry of basements.
Small doors with (seemingly unnecessarily)
sturdy hardware heading under stairs.
A trapezoid of a green door
carved out of stone,
four feet up the wall—with no stairs going to it.

Doors promise a passage; but,
they are not windows. Windows'
transparency preclude real mystery. They
provide cheap knowledge.
A door is mystery, a veil
to be lifted, and how childish to believe
all mysteries benevolent. A door demands
blood.

Niceties

What if,
instead of a bland,
prosaic, formality, your
"Have a good day" were
an earnest, deep,
Prayer?

Human Hearts

Pulse

Under golden skin
Delicate, transparent blossoms or
Ripened patent red apples,
Dark boughs tangled wet
Shining silver
Rainbow iridescence
Soft slow soothing

Pulse

Fate

The call of the midnight train sounds out
across the empty fields until deflected
by the buffeting limbs of trees. It ricochets over
head sweeping the wheel of the harmonious heavens,
until the dislodged stars dribble into the narrow opening
of the black river beside us. We convene at a crossroads—
as lovers do. Love is free
will because it compels choice.
We choose not to hear the call;
we care nothing for drowned stars.

Acknowledgements

The cover photo for *Cold Songs* was provided by the talented photographer Karl Guth. Karl was recently taken from us by pancreatic cancer and his wife Collette Guth has graciously allowed the reproduction of this image.

The following poems previously appeared in *Prairie Gold: An Anthology of the American Heartland* and are reprinted here with kind permission of the Ice Cube Press, LLC: "Love on the Plains," "More," "White."

The author wishes to thank Steve Semken and Lance Sacknoff for their support and superb editorial skills.

Dometa Wiegand Brothers is a native of the north woods of Wisconsin. She holds a BA and an MSTE from the University of Wisconsin Stevens Point and a PhD from Washington State University. She has taught at universities in Wisconsin, Washington, Idaho, Alabama, and Iowa.

She is the author of the scholarly monograph *On All Sides Infinity*, as well as numerous articles and book chapters. Her poetry has also been anthologized in *Prairie Gold: An Anthology of the American Heartland*.

Dometa Wiegand Brothers currently lives and writes in central Iowa.